THE PORTABLE **7** HABITS™

Renewal

Nourishing Body, Mind, Heart, and Soul

THE **7** HABITS
OF HIGHLY EFFECTIVE PEOPLE ®

Other Books from Franklin Covey
Choice: Choosing the Proactive Life You Want to Live
The 7 Habits of Highly Effective People
The 7 Habits of Highly Effective Families
The 7 Habits of Highly Effective Teens
The 7 Habits of Highly Effective Teens Journal
Daily Reflections for Highly Effective People
Living the 7 Habits
Loving Reminders for Kids
Loving Reminders for Couples
Loving Reminders for Families
Loving Reminders Teen to Teen
Quotes and Quips

Franklin Covey
2200 West Parkway Boulevard
Salt Lake City, Utah 84119-2099

©1999 by Franklin Covey Co. 9904002

Concept: Cheryl Kerzner
Design: Jenny Peterson
Illustration: Tammy Smith
Editing: Sunny Larson and Debra Harris
Contributors: Sunny Larson, Debra Harris, Lynn Frost, Lyn Christian, Reid Later, Crickett Willardsen, Matthew Clyde, Judy Ball, Todd Davis, Holli Karren, Donelle Deinstadt, Shelley Orgill

Manufactured in United States of America

ISBN 1-929494-03-3

CONTENTS

Have you noticed how awe is a reaction to the daily magic of life? When we are too busy to stop in awe, we may be too busy to live. Awe means stopping and noticing, and for a slight moment remembering, that we are a part of a vast universe.

—ANNE WILSON SCHAEF

INTRODUCTION

Feeling good doesn't just happen. You can't just snap your fingers and decide to feel good without making a conscious effort. Living a life in balance means taking the necessary time to renew yourself. It is all up to you. You can renew yourself through relaxation. Or you can totally burn yourself out by overdoing everything. You can pamper yourself mentally and spiritually. Or you can go through life oblivious to your well-being. You can experience vibrant energy. Or you can procrastinate and miss out on the benefits of good health. You can revitalize yourself in order to face a new day in peace and harmony. Or you can wake up in the morning full of apathy because your get-up-and-go is long gone. Just remember that every day provides a new opportunity for renewal. A new opportunity to recharge yourself instead of hitting the wall. All it takes is a little time. And the Portable 7 Habits.

In *Renewal: Nourishing Body, Mind, Heart, and Soul* we've simplified the powerful principles behind *The 7 Habits of Highly Effective People* by Stephen R. Covey to help you realize the benefits of living a balanced, more peaceful existence.

There are no roadmaps to follow. No instructions. No how-tos. And no formulas for success. Instead you'll find a collection of thought-provoking questions, inspirational quotes, provocative messages, and practical wisdom.

As you turn these pages, take the words of advice to heart, mind, body, and soul. Think about what you read. Ponder how and what it would take to renew yourself on a more consistent basis. Let the wisdom inspire you to learn, grow, and create new opportunities. Exercise your body as well as your mind. Give yourself permission to be the best you can be. Start shaping your life right now in a more positive light instead of living in the future or worrying about the past. Choose to take time for yourself rather than completely depleting yourself in favor of giving others all they demand.

In essence, make it a habit to sharpen the saw.

HABIT 7: SHARPEN THE SAW®

Renew yourself on a regular basis.

BALANCE

Habit 7 is taking time to sharpen the saw...It's preserving and enhancing the greatest asset you have—you. It's renewing the four dimensions of your nature—physical, spiritual, mental, and social/emotional...This is the single most powerful investment we can ever make in life—investment in ourselves, in the only instrument we have with which to deal with life and to contribute.

—STEPHEN R. COVEY, *The 7 Habits of Highly Effective People*

BALANCE

is the key to success in all things. Do not neglect your mind, body or spirit. Invest time and energy in all of them equally—it will be the best investment you ever make, not just for your life but for whatever is to follow.

—TANYA WHEWAY

What can you do to live a more balanced life?

Everyone is a house with four rooms:

PHYSICAL
MENTAL
EMOTIONAL
SPIRITUAL

Unless we go into every room every day,
even if only to keep it aired,
we are not a complete person.

—RUMER GODDEN

If you could choose

5

things to do outside of work that would nourish your soul, what would they be?

Your thorns are the best part of you.

——MARIANNE MOORE

Don't evaluate your life in terms of achievements, trivial or monumental, along the way. If you do, you will be destined to the frustration of always seeking out other destinations, and never allowing yourself actually to be fulfilled…Instead,

WAKE UP

and appreciate everything you encounter along your path. Enjoy the flowers that are there for your pleasure. Tune in to the sunrise, the little children, the laughter, the rain and the birds. Drink it all in…there is no way to happiness; happiness IS the way.

—WAYNE W. DYER

There must be more to life than having everything.

—MAURICE SENDAK

You must learn day by day, year by year, to broaden your horizons. The more things you love, the more you are interested in, the more you enjoy, the more you are indignant about, the more you have left when anything happens.

—ETHEL BARRYMORE

To laugh is to risk appearing the fool.

To weep is to risk appearing sentimental.

To reach for another is to risk involvement.

To expose your feelings is to risk exposing your true self.

To place your ideas, your dreams before a crowd is to risk their loss.

To love is to risk not being loved in return.

To live is to risk dying.

To believe is to risk despair.

To try is to risk failure.

But risks must be taken, because the greatest hazard in life is to risk nothing.

They may avoid suffering and sorrow, but they cannot learn, feel, change, grow, love, live.

Chained by their attitudes they are slaves; they have forfeited their freedom.

Only a person who risks is free.

—ANONYMOUS CHICAGO TEACHER

You have to decide what your highest priorities are and have the courage—pleasantly, smilingly, nonapologetically—to say "no" to other things. And the way you do that is by having a bigger "yes" burning inside.

The enemy of the best is often the good.

—STEPHEN R. COVEY

What is CLUTTERING your life?

What keeps you awake at night?

Of all the judgments we pass in life, none is more important than the judgment we pass on ourselves.

——NATHANIEL BRANDON

HEALTH

Probably the greatest benefit you will experience from exercising will be the development of your Habit 1 muscles of proactivity. As you act based on the value of physical well-being instead of reacting to all the forces that keep you from exercising, your paradigm of yourself, your self-esteem, your self-confidence, and your integrity will be profoundly affected.

——STEPHEN R. COVEY, *The 7 Habits of Highly Effective People*

Walk, run, bike, jump, dance, swim, play.

But don't stop there. Exercise your rights as a human being. Exercise your faith. Do it often, then do it again. Exercise your right to be treated with dignity, and help others to exercise theirs. Exercise your brain so it doesn't get flabby. Figure out a problem. Take a stab at a crossword puzzle, learn a new language. Better yet, learn an ancient language. Try to guess "whodunit" before the end of the show. Exercise your heart without ever getting on the stairs. Feel the burn when you love someone who seems not at all lovely. Stretch your heart muscles so it can open wider and stay open longer. Exercise your emotions by getting them in motion. Can you still cry when you see something tender? Are your lips toned enough to break into a broad smile at the sight of something sweet? Exercise your humanity: use it or lose it.

—RACHEL SNYDER

What did you enjoy doing as a child ?

A strong body/personality structure is not created by eating certain foods, doing certain exercises, or following anybody's rules or good ideas. It is created by trusting your intuition and **learning to follow its direction.**

—SHAKTI GAWAIN

Your body will honor you with wellness if you honor it with awareness.

PEOPLE WHO CANNOT FIND TIME

FOR RECREATION ARE OBLIGED

SOONER OR LATER TO FIND TIME

FOR ILLNESS.

——JOHN WANAMAKER

Remember a time when you were *truly happy.*

What did it feel like? How can you feel like that again?

FORGET SUPERMODELS.

If more people could look like them,
they wouldn't be called super.

FORGET MANNEQUINS.

They're made in factories,
not in gene pools dripping with wide hips and flabby arms.

——SANDY WEINSTEIN

Most of us think we don't have enough time to exercise. Talk about a distorted perspective! We don't have time not to. When your car is running out of gas, do you just keep on driving and say, "I don't have time to fill up"?

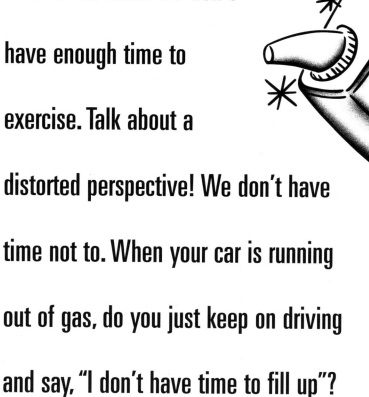

$\mathcal{Y}$our body is your gift
however imperfect
it may be.

Treat it with love.

It's not about weight, it's about caring for yourself on a daily basis. Renew! Renew! Renew!

—OPRAH WINFREY

I've been on a constant diet for the last two decades. I've lost a total of 789 pounds. By all accounts, I should be hanging from a charm bracelet.

—ERMA BOMBECK

HEART

Where does intrinsic security come from? It doesn't come from what other people think of us or how they treat us. It doesn't come from the scripts they've handed us. It doesn't come from our circumstances or our position. It comes from deep within. It comes from accurate paradigms and correct principles deep in our own mind and heart. It comes from inside-out congruence, from living a life of integrity in which our daily habits reflect our deepest values.

——STEPHEN R. COVEY, *The 7 Habits of Highly Effective People*

*L*et me hold you in my heart, my soul, and in my dreams...
experiencing you in my mind...for loving you has given me
the power to know who I really am.

—SHARON WARREN

What can you do today to express your love?

STOP
looking for Prince
Charming.

Cinderella's already got him.

—ILENE BECKERMAN

There is a specific point at which you shift from being recently single to really single. It comes when you have heard this piece of advice more than twice: "Well, you have to get OUT THERE." At first it sort of means something to you. "Yes," you think, "that's right. That's my problem. I have to get out there." This occurs immediately before you find yourself unable to answer the question: "Out where?" And of course the people who gave you this advice cannot tell you where OUT THERE is. They have no idea. They are the same people who probably also said to you, "One door closes. Another door opens." "What door?" you probably wondered. The door that goes OUT THERE.

—MERRILL MARKOE

The most important ingredient

we put into any relationship,

is not what we say or what we do,

but what we are.

—STEPHEN R. COVEY

How can you

STRENGTHEN YOUR RELATIONSHIP

with a significant other?

Only perfect people find the perfect mate.
—BETH MENDY CONNY

Taking Initiative in Relationships

If you're a woman, and you want to have a successful relationship with a guy, the Number One Tip to remember is:

Never assume that the guy understands that you and he have a relationship. The guy will not realize this on his own. You have to plant the idea in his brain by constantly making subtle references to it in your everyday conversation, such as:

> "Roger, would you mind passing me a Sweet 'n' Low, inasmuch as we have a relationship?"

> "Wake up, Roger! There's a prowler in the den and we have a relationship! You and I do, I mean."

> "Good News, Roger! The gynecologist says we're going to have our fourth child, which will serve as yet another indication that we have a relationship!"

> "Roger, inasmuch as this plane is crashing and we probably have only about a minute to live, I want you to know that we've had a wonderful fifty-three years of marriage together, which clearly constitutes a relationship."

Never let up, women. Pound away relentlessly at this concept, and eventually it will start to penetrate the guy's brain. Some day he might even start thinking about it on his own. He'll be talking with some other guys about women, and, out of the blue, he'll say, "Elaine and I, we have, ummm... We have, ahhh... We...We have this thing." And he will sincerely mean it.

—DAVE BARRY

Being the one who

always has to be

"right"

in your dealings with

others can mean you

have fewer meaningful

relationships.

THE EMOTIONAL BANK ACCOUNT

Meaningful relationships are not like the mold accumulating on the fontina in your fridge. They require conscious effort. Each relationship is like a bank account. The quality of the relationship depends upon what you put into it. Keeping promises, being courteous and kind, offering support, listening, and taking time for the other person are just a few ways to make deposits. Of course there are certain things that will make withdrawals, and you'll want to minimize those. Keep your Emotional Bank Accounts growing, and you'll see the dividends in deeper, more meaningful relationships.

Where does your heart lead you?

INSPIRATION

The more we can see people in terms of their unseen potential, the more we can use our imagination rather than our memory, with our spouse, our children, our coworkers or employees. We can refuse to label them—we can "see" them in new fresh ways each time we're with them. We can help them become independent, fulfilled people capable of deeply satisfying, enriching and productive relationships with others.

——STEPHEN R. COVEY, *The 7 Habits of Highly Effective People*

*I*nspiration is the
gentle listening
to the wisdom of
our inner being.

—ANNE WILSON SCHAEF

INSPIRATION
CANNOT BE FORCED.

Sometimes it simply comes like a bolt out of the blue; at other times it totally refuses to come out to play. There are times, however, when we can cajole it into action by freeing our minds—listening to some beautiful music, spending time in a beautiful garden, meditating, reading, exposing ourselves to a new environment or spending time with positive, passionate and creative people.

——TANYA WHEWAY

Practice the
Platinum Rule:
Do unto others
as they want to be done to.

what inspires you?

If

you've gotten in touch with your higher self,

perfected your mantra,

played with your inner child,

revisited your past lives,

rebirthed,

rebreathed and recapitulated your rage,

wailed for the weekend,

bared your soul for the masses,

and experienced hot coals for wholeness,

get a reality check.

There's got to be a 12-Step Program for
self-help addicts somewhere.

What memories can you pass on

to your children about your ancestors? What are you doing so that your family remembers you?

What makes life worth

BE WILLING

to take the first step, no matter how small it is. Concentrate on the fact that you are willing to learn. Absolute miracles will happen.

—LOUISE L. HAY

If you don't experience your life, you're not going to come up with solutions for everything. Every intention, every achievement has come out of dissatisfaction, not serenity. No one ever said, "Things are perfect. Let's invent fire."

—FRAN LEBOWITZ

KINDNESS

There is an intrinsic security that comes from service, from helping other people in a meaningful way. One important source is your work, when you see yourself in a contributive and creative mode, really making a difference. Another source is anonymous service—no one knows it and no one necessarily will. And that's not the concern; the concern is blessing the lives of other people. Influence, not recognition, becomes the motive.

——STEPHEN R. COVEY, *The 7 Habits of Highly Effective People*

Kind words can be short and easy to speak,
but their echoes are truly endless.

—MOTHER TERESA

What one act
of kindness
can you do
EVERY day?

My religion is very simple.
My religion is kindness.
—DALAI LAMA

Three things in human
life are important.

The first is to
be kind,
the second is to
be kind,
and the third is to
be kind.

—HENRY JAMES

I wanted a perfect ending.

Now I've learned, the hard way, that some

poems don't rhyme and some stories don't have

a clear beginning, middle and end. Life is about

not knowing, having to change, taking the

moment and making the best of it, without

knowing what's going to happen next.

Delicious ambiguity.

——GILDA RADNER

Let us be grateful to people who make us happy;
they are the charming gardeners
who make our souls blossom.

—MARCEL PROUST

57

When was the last time you really listened and took interest in another person?

Life loves to be taken

by the hand and be told,

"I am with you, kid.

Let's go."

—MAYA ANGELOU

Hostility drains you.

Kindness fills you up.

MIND

Education—continuing education, continually honing and expanding the mind—is vital mental renewal. Sometimes that involves the external discipline of the classroom or systematized study programs; more often it does not. Proactive people can figure out many, many ways to educate themselves. It is extremely valuable to train the mind to stand apart and examine its own program. That, to me, is the definition of a liberal education—the ability to examine the programs of life against larger questions and purposes and other paradigms.

——STEPHEN R. COVEY, *The 7 Habits of Highly Effective People*

In the end, everyone is

our teacher, our friends,

our family, the stranger

on the street. Every

experience is a challenge;

a teaching is always

hidden in it. Every

thought that bubbles up

in our minds can teach

us things about

ourselves,

if we are able to learn.

—DAVID A. COOPER

When was the last time you really checked in with yourself?

I LEARN

by going where I have to go.

—THEODORE ROETHKE

Keep learning about the world.

Use your mind to the hilt. Life passes quickly and, towards the end, gathers speed like a freight train running downhill. The more you know, the more you enrich yourself and others.

—SUSAN TROTT

After a while you learn the difference between

holding a hand and chaining a soul.

And you learn that love doesn't mean security.

You begin to learn that kisses aren't contracts

and presents aren't promises

And you begin to accept your defeats with

your head up and eyes open

And with the grace of an adult, not the grief of a child.

You learn to travel all the roads on today,

Because tomorrow's ground is too uncertain for your plans.

After a while you learn that even the sunshine

burns if you get too much.

So plant your own garden and decorate your own soul

Instead of waiting for someone to bring you flowers.

You will learn that you really can endure,

That you really are special

And that you really do have worth.

So live to learn and know yourself. In doing so you will

learn to live.

—ANONYMOUS

What gives your spirit, mind, heart, and body energy

I say if it's going to be done, let's do it. Let's not put it in the hands of fate. Let's not put it in the hands of someone who doesn't know me. I know me best. Then take a breath and go ahead.

—ANITA BAKER

What to do when you're
READY TO LOSE YOUR MIND.

GET SOME OXYGEN.

Focused breathing can help you control your physical responses to stress. Put your tongue on the roof of your mouth behind your teeth, inhale deeply through your nose, and fill up with air until your stomach sticks out like a baby's. Then slowly release the air through your nose or mouth. Do this at least 3 times. It will help you to loosen up and settle down.

TAKE A PERSPECTIVE CHECK.

Get the big picture quick by asking yourself: Okay, will I care about this in a month? In a year? If you're going to freak out, make sure it's for a good reason. If your reason for stressing suddenly seems ridiculous, laugh it off.

CHOOSE YOUR RESPONSE.

Pick the appropriate and productive emotion: anger, courage, humor, compassion, sadness, or whatever. Any emotion is okay as long as you remain in control and handle the situation with a little finesse.

why not?

learn to draw

subscribe to a new magazine

delegate   write in a daily journal

take up a hobby   volunteer

control your temper

join a chess club

purchase a book of word puzzles

turn the radio off on your way to and from work

take a class

plan a walk in the midafternoon to refresh your thinking

learn another language

join a book club

learn to restore furniture

repair a bike

start bird watching

learn to take pictures

try guided visualizations

listen to soothing music

70

Do you remember the delight in finding a crab at the seashore or blowing bubbles with a pink wand? What would reignite the childlike sense of wonder you once possessed?

What is your vision?

RENEWAL

Balanced renewal is optimally synergetic. The things you do to sharpen the saw in any one dimension have positive impact in other dimensions because they are so highly interrelated. Your physical health affects your mental health; your spiritual strength affects your social/emotional strength. As you improve in one dimension, you increase your ability in other dimensions as well.

—STEPHEN R. COVEY, *The 7 Habits of Highly Effective People*

Sharpening the Saw

Suppose you were to come upon someone in the woods working feverishly
to saw down a tree.

"What are you doing?" you ask.

"Can't you see?" comes the impatient reply. "I'm sawing down this tree."

"You look exhausted!" you exclaim. "How long have you been at it?"

"Over five hours," he returns, "and I'm beat! This is hard work."

**"Well why don't you take a break for a few minutes and sharpen the saw?"
you inquire. "I'm sure it would go a lot faster."**

"I don't have time to sharpen the saw," the man says emphatically.
"I'm too busy sawing."

—STEPHEN R. COVEY

*S*poiling yourself every once in awhile
is actually good for you. It triggers endorphins.
It's satisfying. You don't have to throw down
the self-discipline gauntlet, just relax a little.
Indulging can help you control cravings so they
don't turn into binge-fests. Balance is about
enjoying bliss, not just cutting out the junk.

$\mathcal{I}$nside myself is a place where I live all alone and that's where you renew your springs that never dry up.

—PEARL S. BUCK

Renewal is the principle and the process that empowers us to move on an upward spiral of growth and change, of continuous improvement.

—STEPHEN R. COVEY

A Self-Renewal Plan

START SMALL. Start your plan with an activity that you feel very motivated doing and is also easily accomplished.

KEEP IT GOING. Continue using any successful activity you're already doing for renewal.

TAKE YOUR TIME. Play with different ideas and experiment until you find the combination of things that work for you.

DON'T OVERWHELM YOURSELF. If all of your renewal activities fill daily time slots, you could become overwhelmed rather than enlivened.

CONTINUALLY ADJUST. Very rarely will a plan work forever. Plan to continually adjust and update your activities.

BE SELF-AWARE. Your likes, dislikes, and personal style will help you in planning activities, which yield your greatest restorative potential.

What are you trying to accomplish?

Are you willing to change the way you play the game?

Five Steps to Inner Renewal

REMEMBER

Buried under the years and experiences of your life is a memory of a dream, a forgotten wanting, a simple whim. Capture the memory once again and make it a reality.

CREATE

Sometimes we are afraid to express ourselves in a way that leaves tangible evidence of our thoughts and feelings. Create something, even if you start by revisiting a box of Crayolas.

ABSORB

Often what you have is what you've chosen to have. There must be something about your "now" that you can be fully glad is yours. Maybe it is a sunset, a flower garden, a favorite piece of music. Allow yourself to absorb one gift that's yours.

WANT

If you never felt the discomfort of thirst, your body would dry up. The wanting inside of you should be honored like thirst. What is it? What do you want? Drink it up. Find a way to put the wanting at peace. Then listen for the next want. Quenching wants nurtures your soul.

NEED

We often neglect our needs as much as we do our wants. A need is deeper than a want. If you need rest, take it. If you need laughter, create it. If you need love, grow it.

Now don't get me wrong: You can howl all you want, just don't expect to get whole in this lifetime. Because the truth is, no matter how much you wail and flail and get in touch with the incredible inner you, you're not going to get completely whole because the only people who are completely whole are also completely dead. **Do you want to be like them?**

—BARBARA GRAHAM

LIFE
is not orderly.

No matter how we try to

make life so, right in the

middle of it we die,

lose a leg, fall in love,

drop a jar of applesauce.

—NATALIE GOLDBERG

If you find you are not feeling in love anymore, be more loving.

—FRANK PITTMAN III

SANCTUARY

Someone once inquired of a Far Eastern Zen master, who had a great serenity and peace about him no matter what pressures he faced, "How do you maintain that serenity and peace?" He replied, "I never leave my place of meditation." He meditated early in the morning and for the rest of the day, he carried the peace of those moments with him in his mind and heart.

—STEPHEN R. COVEY, *The 7 Habits of Highly Effective People*

Your Own Little
Sanctuary

Is your home a place of refuge or just a nagging reminder that carpets do indeed require regular vacuuming? Here are a few things you can do to make it a place you want to come home to.

Splurge on fresh flowers every once in awhile.
They brighten your home and can smell wonderful. Even a bunch of daisies in a glass can create a sense of serenity.

Turn on some beautiful music.
It can change your mood and helps you to wind down, relax, and regroup.

Have a clean-up bin.
Pick up clutter and put it in a sort-through-later bin. A clean room can make your surroundings more peaceful.

Try some aromatherapy.
It's not hard to get your hands on scented candles, oils, sachets, or sprays. A wonderful smell can be truly soothing.

Reap the benefits of live plants.
Plants can help to hydrate your skin, lower blood pressure, and reduce dust and indoor chemical pollutants. And they look nice.

My favorite thing is to go where I've never been.

—DIANE ARBUS

privacy is essential

not only to the souls of painters and poets, who thrive in solitude,

but to the rest of us, too—individuals whose canvas is our lives.

—SUE HALPERN

Within you is a stillness

and a sanctuary to

which you can retreat

at any time and

be yourself.

—HERMAN HESSE

Too much metal.
Too much fat.
Too many jokes.
Not enough meditation.

—ALLEN GINSBERG

If you could build **your very own retreat**

what would it look like? How would you use it?

Can you come out and play?

The sharing of joy, whether physical, emotional, psychic or intellectual, forms a bridge between the sharers which can be the basis for understanding much of what is not shared between them, and lessens the threat of their difference.

—AUDRE LORDE

Take sanctuary in small things:

an ice cream cone

laughing

hot baths

a good movie

bare feet

a hug

kissing a baby

a leaf

candlelight

SIMPLICITY

I believe that a life of integrity is the most fundamental source of personal worth. I do not agree with the popular success literature that says that self-esteem is primarily a matter of mind set, of attitude—that you can psych yourself into peace of mind. Peace of mind comes when your life is in harmony with true principles and values and in no other way.

—STEPHEN R. COVEY, *The 7 Habits of Highly Effective People*

CELEBRATE

the ordinary.

Whatever happened to stopping and smelling the roses?

Duke bounds out of bed at seven in the morning. "Gotta run," he says hurriedly kissing me goodbye. "I've got a breakfast meeting.

"Remember the good old days when we used to have breakfast meetings in bed?" I ask wistfully.

"I'll call you," Duke promises. And he does call. But I'm at the gym. And when I call back, he's in a meeting. And then I'm doing an interview. And then he's got an important call on the other line. And so it goes. Love in the Time of Telephone Tag.

—MARGO KAUFMAN

4 Easy Ways to Simplify Your Life

SCHEDULE SOME DOWNTIME EVERY DAY
Write in a journal or take a quiet bath before bed.
Recognize that not doing it all is OK—even important.

MAKE A PLAN TO PAY OFF CREDIT CARD BALANCES
Yes, you can do it. Ditch all cards except two—one card for
your business expenses and one for personal expenses.

LEAVE THE TV OFF ONE EVENING A WEEK
You'll be surprised at the extra time you have. Leaving it
off may become a habit.

DON'T BE A SLAVE TO THE PHONE
Let your machine pick up—if it's important, they'll leave you
a message. When you get annoying solicitation calls, ask to
have your name removed from the company's list.

What can you do less of?

What should you do more of?

*L*ife is what happens to you
while you're busy making other plans.

—JOHN LENNON

what is life?

It is the flash of a firefly in the night. It is the breath of a buffalo in the wintertime. It is the little shadow that runs across the grass and loses itself in the sunset.

—CROWFOOT

What is complicating
your life right now?

How can you simplify it?

S I M P L I F Y I N G

is not necessarily about getting rid of everything we've worked so hard for. It's about making wise choices among the things we now have to choose from. It's about recognizing that trying to have it all has gotten in the way of enjoying the things which do add to our happiness and well-being. It's about deciding what's important to us, and gracefully letting go of the things that aren't. Simplifying is not necessarily about moving to Walden Pond and sending the laundry home to mother. It's about simplifying our lives right where we are. It's about learning to reduce the laundering chore, along with all the other chores and frequently self-imposed obligations, so we can begin to make the contributions we all, in our heart of hearts, want to make to our family, to our community, to our environment, and to the world.

——ELAINE ST. JAMES

Are you saying

YES

when you really want to say

NO?

When you slow down you begin to discover there is a silent awareness of what it is that you do not want to look at.

I finally figured out the only reason to be alive is to **enjoy it.**

—RITA MAE BROWN

SOUL

The spiritual dimension is your core, your center, your commitment to your value system. It's a very private area of life and a supremely important one. It draws upon the sources that inspire and uplift you and tie you to the timeless truths of all humanity...If you win the battles there, if you settle the issues that inwardly conflict, you feel a sense of peace, a sense of knowing what you're about.

——STEPHEN R. COVEY, *The 7 Habits of Highly Effective People*

The soul was never put in the body to stand still.

——JOHN WEBSTER

You are only as powerful as that for which you stand.

Do you stand for more money in the bank and a bigger house? Do you stand for an attractive mate? Do you stand for imposing your way of thinking upon others? These are stands of the personality seeking to satisfy its wants. Do you stand for perfection, for the beauty and compassion of the soul? Do you stand for forgiveness and humbleness? These are the stands of the position of a truly powerful personality.

—GARY ZUKAV

Maybe you've been wandering around and thinking, "There has got to be some kind of level of meaning which exists in other people's lives, which has somehow never revealed itself to me. I see it on their faces; I know that something is there, but I cannot put my finger on it." Okay, you aren't really going to like this, but you know that week you had the flu back in fourth grade, and you came back and everyone seemed "different" to you? That week your entire class was taken to see an Indian Mystic and he completely explained the Whole Shebang to them, and afterwards, they got to have ice cream.

—STEPHANIE BRUSH

Even a thought, even a possibility, can shatter and transform us.

—FRIEDRICH NIETZSCHE

what are you committed to?

Safety is the most unsafe spiritual path you can take. Safety keeps you numb and dead. People are caught by surprise when it is time to die. They have allowed themselves to live so little.

—STEPHEN LEVINE

What is YOUR unique purpose on this earth?

Check the items to which you can truthfully answer "yes".

❑ I have defined what I value and believe. I plan and live my life accordingly.

❑ I have created my own mission statement. I rely on it to give vision to my purpose in life.

❑ I find daily renewal through meditation, prayer, study, or reflection.

❑ I frequently spend time in nature, a synagogue, a chapel, a temple, or someplace where I find spiritual renewal.

❑ I keep my heart open to truth.

❑ I am able to take a stand or tell the truth, even when opposed by others.

❑ I frequently serve others with no expectations of any type of returned favor.

❑ I can identify which things in life I can change and which things I cannot. I let go of the things I cannot change.

❑ I can connect to inspirational guidance as needed.

Almost any intense emotion may open our "inward eye" to the beauty of reality. Falling in love appears to do it for some people. The beauties of nature or the exhilaration of artistic creation does it for others. Probably any high experience may momentarily stretch our souls up on tiptoe, so that we catch a glimpse of that marvelous beauty which is always there, but which we are not often tall enough to perceive.

—MARGERET PRESCOTT MONTAGUE

Be patient

with yourself. Self-growth is tender; it's holy ground.

—STEPHEN R. COVEY

The simple fact remains…that the stronger and more radiant we are, the more we can serve as a positive influence in the world. The more happiness we bring into the world, the better it is for everyone. Happiness (or love) serves as a master key to open every doorway to social progress.

Happy people create happiness; it's the most contagious energy on Earth.

—DAN MILLMAN

About Franklin Covey

Franklin Covey is the world's leading time management and life leadership company. Based on proven principles, our services and products are used by more than 15 million people worldwide. We work with a wide variety of clients, Fortune 500 material, as well as smaller companies, communities, and organizations. You may know us from our world-renowned Franklin Planner or any of our books in the 7 Habits series. By the way, Franklin Covey books have sold over 15 million copies worldwide—over $1\frac{1}{2}$ million each year. But what you may not know about Franklin Covey is we also offer leadership training, motivational workshops, personal coaching, audiotapes and videotapes, and *PRIORITIES* magazine just to name a few.

Let Us Know What You Think

We'd love to hear your suggestions or comments about *Renewal: Nourishing Body, Mind, Heart, and Soul*. And we'll let you know when the other books in The Portable 7 Habits series are available.

www.franklincovey.com/portable7

The Portable 7 Habits
Franklin Covey
MS0733-CK
2200 West Parkway Boulevard
Salt Lake City, Utah 84119-2331 USA

1-800-952-6839
International (801) 229-1333 Fax (801) 229-1233

RECOMMENDED READING

Alexander, Jane. *Spirit of the Home: How to Make Your Home a Sanctuary*. Thorsons Publishing, 1998.

Andes, Karen. *A Woman's Book of Strength: An Empowering Guide to Total Mind/Body Fitness*. Perigree, 1995.

Beattie, Melody. *Codependent No More: How to Stop Controlling Others and Start Caring for Yourself*. Hazeldon Information Education, 1996.

Borysenko, Joan. *Pocketful of Miracles: Prayers, Meditations, and Affirmations to Nurture Your Spirit Every Day of the Year*. Warner Books, 1994.

Cameron, Julia. *The Artist's Way: A Spiritual Path to Higher Creativity*. J. P. Tarcher, 1992.

Carlson, Richard. *Don't Sweat the Small Stuff—and It's All Small Stuff*. Hyperion, 1997.

———— and Wayne Dyer. *You Can Be Happy No Matter What: Five Principles for Keeping Life in Perspective*. New World Library, 1997.

Chodron, Pema. *Start Where You Are: A Guide to Compassionate Living*. Shambhala, 1994.

Covey, Stephen R. *The 7 Habits of Highly Effective People*. Simon & Schuster, 1989.

————. *First Things First: To Live, to Love, to Learn, to Leave a Legacy*. Fireside, 1996.

Csikszentmihaly, Mihaly. *Finding Flow: The Psychology of Engagement with Everyday Life*. Basic Books, 1998.

Hay, Louise L. *101 Ways to Happiness*. Hay House, 1998.

Richardson, Cheryl. *Take Time for Your Life: A Personal Coach's Seven-Step Program for Creating the Life You Want*. Broadway Books, 1998.

Sher, Barbara. *It's Only Too Late if You Don't Start Now: How to Create Your Second Life after Forty*. Delacorte Press, 1998.

———— and Barbara Smith. *I Could Do Anything If I Only Knew What It Was: How to Discover What You Really Want and How to Get It*. Delacorte Press, 1995.

St. James, Elaine. *Simplify Your Life: 100 Ways to Slow Down and Enjoy the Things That Really Matter*. Hyperion, 1994.

Zukav, Gary. *The Seat of the Soul*. Fireside, 1990.